D0583584

Athletes With Disabilities

Athletes With Disabilities

Deborah Kent

Watts LIBRARY™

Franklin Watts
A Division of Scholastic Inc.
New York • Toronto • London • Auckland • Sydney
Mexico City • New Delhi • Hong Kong
Danbury, Connecticut

Note to readers: Definitions for words in **bold** can be found in the Glossary at the back of this book.

Photographs © 2003: AllSport USA/Getty Images: 5 bottom, 34, 36, 37 (Adam Pretty), 32, 50, 51 (Jamie Squire), 31, 32 (Rick Stewart); AP/Wide World Photos: 49 (Mark Duncan), 43 (Douglas C. Pizac), 5 top, 39 (Winslow Townson), 15, 19; CISS: 12; Corbis Images: 41 (AFP), 17, 18 (Bettmann); FPG International/Getty Images/Jim Cummins: cover; Getty Images: 27 (Liaison), 23 (Donald Miralle); Icon Sports Media/John Cordes: 44; Next Step O & P Inc.: 9; Photo Researchers, NY/Lawrence Migdale: 28; PhotoEdit/Robert W.Ginn: 11, 52, 53; Photri Inc./Wachter: 24; Special Olympics, Pennsylvania: 30; SportsChrome USA/Michael Zito: 46, 47; The Image Works/Bob Daemmrich: 2; Tommy Cornille: 6; United States Association of Blind Athletes: 21.

The photograph on the cover shows a young woman winning a wheelchair race. The photograph opposite the title page shows a young man competing in a Special Olympics event.

Library of Congress Cataloging-in-Publication Data

Kent, Deborah
    Athletes with disabilities / by Deborah Kent
       p. cm. — (Watts library)
    Summary: Explores the people and events involved in sports competitions for people with disabilities and discusses people with disabilities who play professional sports.
    Includes bibliographical references and index.
    ISBN 0-531-12019-8 (lib. bdg.)   0-531-16664-3 (pbk.)
    1. Sports for people with disabilities—Juvenile literature. 2. Athletes with disabilities—Biography—Juvenile literature. [1. Sports for people with disabilities. 2. People with disabilities. 3. Athletes.] I. Title. II. Series.
GV709.3 K46 2003
371.9'04486—dc21   2002008883

Contents

With a little help from his prosthesis, Tommy Cornille has been able to play soccer.

Chapter One

The Love of the Game

When Tommy Cornille was seven years old, his mother signed him up to play with a junior soccer team. At first Tommy's father was dismayed. He knew Tommy wanted to play soccer, but he was afraid the game was too fast and rough for him. When he went to watch Tommy at a practice, however, his doubts disappeared. Tommy held his own with the other kids on his team. He played so well that no one could guess he had an artificial leg.

Tommy was born with a condition known as **congenital amputation**, or limb loss from birth. His right leg ends just below the knee. "His disability never has to hold him back," a doctor told the Cornilles when Tommy was four months old. "The only restrictions he'll have are the ones we place upon him." When Tommy began crawling, he relied heavily on his arms to pull himself forward. Even at ten months of age he started to develop exceptional upper-body strength, and his parents suspected he might have talent as an athlete.

When he was less than a year old, Tommy was fitted with his first artificial limb, or **prosthesis**. His prosthesis was replaced routinely as he grew. To encourage him to wear his "helper leg" when he was small, his mother let him decorate each new one with pictures. First it was Mickey Mouse, later a stegosaurus. Later still came cowboys, the Chicago Bulls, and soccer emblems. Wearing his prosthesis, Tommy learned to walk, jump, and run.

After he joined the soccer team, sports became Tommy's life. In the next few years he played baseball and basketball and learned to wrestle. His lightweight plastic prosthesis took quite a beating, and often got cracked and broken. When he was twelve, Tommy got his first athletic prosthesis, an extra-strong leg to wear on the field. The heavy pounding of soccer or basketball games sometimes took its toll. Once, to the amazement of the opposing players, Tommy's foot snapped off in the middle of a soccer match. At halftime his mother rushed to a nearby hardware store. She showed the damaged

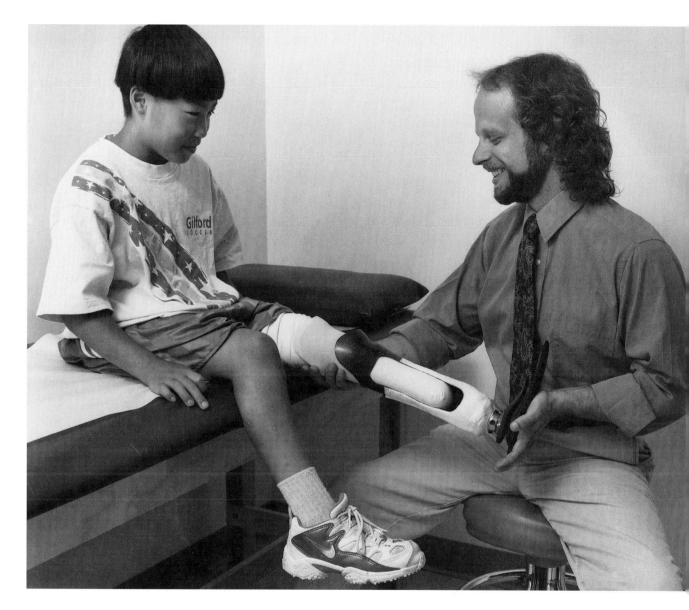

prosthesis to the man behind the counter and explained that she needed a heavy-duty screw to replace the one that had sheared off. Three salespeople worked on the leg and patched it back together with a screw and plenty of epoxy glue. Tommy returned to the game, and his team won.

A child visits a specialist to get fitted for a prosthetic leg.

9

A Choice of Words

Many terms have been used to describe people who differ mentally or physically from the norm. Words such as "crippled," "handicapped," and "impaired" have largely dropped out of usage because they suggest something negative and pitiable. Likewise the phrase "confined to a wheelchair" is no longer widely accepted. A wheelchair is not confining but actually enables one to move about. Many people prefer the terms "physically or mentally challenged" or "differently abled," contending that they carry a neutral, or even favorable, meaning. In the 1980s the terms "disabled" and "people with disabilities" were adopted by groups representing people with a broad range of disabling conditions. Wherever possible, it is best to use "people-first" language—to speak of "a boy who is blind" or a "woman with one hand" rather than a "blind boy" or a "one-handed woman." In this way we think of the person first and see the disability as merely a characteristic of who the person really is.

Tommy Cornille plays goalie with the Raptors, the under-fourteen soccer team in his hometown of Park Ridge, Illinois. He is also a pitcher for his Little League team and plays with the Traveling All-Stars. Coaches say he has quick reaction time, and they marvel at his understanding of the games he plays. "He turns the game inside out to understand it," his father explains. "He's extremely astute. He really uses strategy. He's not quite as fast a runner as some kids, but he makes up for it by using his head."

People often assume that an athlete must have a perfect body, completely free from any disability. Thousands of people the world over are proving that this is not the case. People with amputated limbs, people who use wheelchairs, people who are blind or deaf, and those with a host of other disabilities are involved in every sport imaginable. Like all athletes, they approach sports with ingenuity, determination, and a sense of fun. They get involved for the same reasons that inspire nondisabled athletes—the love of a challenge, the pleasure of teamwork, the simple need to be active. As Tommy Cornille puts it, "If I couldn't play sports I'd get bored. I don't like to just sit around. I've got to get up and do something—that's when I feel really happy."

Like all athletes, people with disabilities enjoy the competition and friendships found in playing sports.

Since the creation of the Silent Games, there have been many sporting events for the deaf. This photograph shows a women's basketball game at the Deaflympics in 2001.

Chapter Two

Beating the Odds

In 1924, thousands of spectators filled a stadium in Paris. They had gathered for a landmark event in the history of athletic competition, the first International Silent Games for the Deaf. During the opening ceremony the organizers of the Games gave a series of speeches. Some addressed the crowd by **signing**, and interpreters delivered their words in spoken French to the hearing members of the audience. Others spoke aloud, and interpreters conveyed their words by signing.

The Silent Games of 1924 was the world's first international competition for disabled athletes. Deaf athletes represented nine European nations, including France, Belgium, The Netherlands, Poland, and the United Kingdom. The motto for the Silent Games, "Equality Through Sport," is just as meaningful today as it was in 1924. Through their commitment to sports of all kinds, athletes with disabilities strive for equality in every sphere of life.

Breaking the Mold

Baseball umpires use a system of hand gestures to communicate with players across the field about balls and strikes. These gestures, part of baseball's heritage, date back to 1889, when a young outfielder named William Hoy signed on with the Washington Nationals. Hoy, who was **profoundly** deaf, taught the umpires to use a purely visual method of communication. Hoy played with the Nationals for fourteen seasons. During one memorable game he threw out three base runners at home plate, a feat no other player has matched to date. Throughout his life Hoy was revered by baseball fans. In

The Jackie Robinson of the Deaf

Many deaf activists argue that William Hoy belongs in the Baseball Hall of Fame in Cooperstown, New York. They feel that Hoy did for deaf players what Jackie Robinson did for players who are African American. A pioneer in the late 1800s, Hoy broke down barriers of prejudice and misunderstanding, and became the first member of his minority to play in the major leagues.

William Hoy throws out the first pitch at the opening of the national league season. Months later, he would toss out the first pitch at a World Series game.

1961, at the age of ninety-nine, he threw out the ceremonial first pitch in the third World Series game between the New York Yankees and the Cincinnati Reds.

Since the earliest days of amateur and professional athletics, people with disabilities have reached the highest ranks. Some managed to make a spectacular comeback after becoming disabled through an illness or injury. Others, such as William Hoy, were disabled from birth or childhood. Despite their disabilities, they entered competitive sports and worked their way to the top.

Grover Cleveland Alexander began his baseball career in the minor leagues as a nondisabled player. As a result of an accident, he developed double vision. Then, when the United States entered World War I in 1917, Alexander joined the army and fought in the trenches of France. Heavy shelling damaged his hearing. Exposure to poisonous mustard gas resulted in **epilepsy**, a disorder that sometimes caused him to have convulsions. Nevertheless, despite his three disabilities, Alexander returned to baseball after the war. Between 1918 and 1929 he played professionally, first with the Chicago Cubs and then with the St. Louis Cardinals.

During World War II, President Franklin D. Roosevelt was eager to keep up the nation's morale. Though most non-disabled men had joined the fighting, Roosevelt insisted that baseball must go on. Professional teams became more open to recruiting players with disabilities. Pete Gray, who lost his right arm in a childhood accident, played for a year with a

baseball team called the St. Louis Browns. Gray batted one-handed and played the outfield. After catching the ball with his gloved hand, he threw the glove into the air, then snatched the ball from the air and hurled it to the infield. He developed this technique as a boy, practicing for hours by throwing rocks and hitting them with a stick.

A more recent major-league baseball player who played one-handed is Jim Abbott. In 1988 Abbot went to the Olympic Games in Seoul, South Korea, where he pitched for the U.S. team in a gold medal game against Japan. Abbott was

Pete Gray showed the world that it was possible to excel at playing baseball with only one hand.

Adversity or Advantage?

For some sports stars a disability has proved to be a real advantage in the game. Mordecai Brown, who played with the Chicago Cubs from 1904 to 1912, befuddled opposing hitters by throwing curveballs with his right hand, from which two fingers were missing. Three fingers were all he needed to throw a wicked curve, and he was nicknamed "Three-Finger" Brown. In 1970 Tom Dempsey kicked the longest field goal in NFL history for the New Orleans Saints. Dempsey, who was born with a partially formed right foot, developed a unique personal style of kicking that amazed his fans.

drafted by the California Angels in 1988 without ever playing in the minor leagues.

Athletes with disabilities began to make their mark in Olympic competition after World War II. A Hungarian named Karoly Tacasz represented his country in marksmanship, shooting left-handed after he lost his right arm. Lisel Hartel of Denmark was the first wheelchair user to compete in the Olympics. In 1952 she won a silver medal for **dressage**, an elaborate style of horseback riding, in the Olympic Games in Helsinki, Finland.

Lisel Hartel (left) rides her horse Jubilee around the stadium at an equestrian event.

Only a handful of athletes, with or without disabilities, ever play on professional teams or compete in the Olympics. For millions of others, local and national organizations offer the opportunity to compete and have fun. Today a host of organizations provide athletic opportunities for people with disabilities.

Something for Everyone

Special competitions for deaf athletes began in Berlin in 1888 and spread to other European countries over the decades that followed. Six national associations for deaf athletes were formed in Europe between 1888 and 1924. The United States first entered the World Games for the Deaf in 1935.

Yet it was not until World War II that people with other disabilities began to form athletic organizations. Doctors working with wounded veterans realized that their patients could benefit by taking part in sports. Athletics became part of the **rehabilitation**, program designed to bring these veterans back into society and the job market. Sponsored by a leading rehabilitation hospital, the first Stoke-Mandeville Games were held in Aylesbury, England, in 1948. The participants, all wheelchair users, competed in basketball, archery, rugby, tennis, and marksmanship. At about the same time the first wheelchair basketball games for U.S. veterans were held in Corona, California.

During the 1950s wheelchair sports expanded to include nonveterans. In 1960 the first Paralympic Summer Games for

people with spinal-cord injuries were held in Rome. The Paralympic Games are held every four years in the same city as the Olympics.

Meanwhile, other disability groups formed their own organizations and hosted local, national, and international competitions in a variety of events. The United States Association of Blind Athletes (USABA) was formed in 1976. The year 1978 saw the establishment of the **Cerebral Palsy** International

Kevin Szott (right), an athlete who is blind, battles his opponent in the Judo competition at The Paralympic Games in Sydney, Australia. He won the gold medal for this event.

Sports and Recreation Association (CPISRA), and the International Sports Federation for Persons with Mental Handicaps was chartered in the Netherlands in 1986. People of small stature formed the Dwarf Athletic Association of the United States in 1989.

Disabled veterans organized Disabled Sports USA (DSUSA) in California in 1987. DSUSA teaches downhill skiing to people with disabilities and creates opportunities in a variety of other sports, from hang gliding to white-water rafting. The organization's motto captures the philosophy of many people with disabilities who become involved in sports: "If I can do this, I can do anything."

The most outstanding athletes from these and other organizations are selected to compete in the Paralympics. Modeled on the Olympics, the Paralympics include both summer and winter games. Athletes compete in categories based on gender and disability. The result is a complex set of divisions and sub-divisions that may bewilder a newcomer. There are seven classes for spinal cord-injured wheelchair-users, eight classes for people with cerebral palsy, three classes for blind people, and twelve classes for amputees. These groupings attempt to match competitors who have similar degrees of disability. Thus partially blind people compete with others who have partial vision, totally blind people play against others who are totally blind, people who have lost both legs compete with other double amputees, and so on.

Like athletes in the regular Olympics, Paralympians strive for bronze, silver, and gold medals. Their prizes are a tribute to their true athletic achievements. They are **elite**, or top-level, athletes dedicated to reaching the heights of physical performance.

A Canadian athlete competes in the Men's Giant Slalom during the Salt Lake City Winter Paralympic Games in 2002.

The Special Olympics has offered people with mental retardation an opportunity to compete in sporting events since 1968.

Chapter Three

Brave in the Attempt

*"I first started in the Special Olympics
when I was twelve years old. My mom had
some problems. She sent me to school and
said she did not want me anymore. Special
Olympics makes me believe in myself."*

—La Bryon Barton,
Special Olympics athlete

Up and Moving

When John F. Kennedy became president of the United States in 1961, he
made an announcement that startled the

nation. He declared that one of his **priorities** was to improve the lives of people with **mental retardation**. He explained that he had a special interest in this area due to the disability of one of his sisters, Rosemary.

In the early 1960s many parents felt ashamed when they had a child with mental retardation. Doctors often advised families to put children with retardation in institutions and pretend they had never been born. Kennedy's announcement brought the topic of mental retardation into the open at last.

One of the president's sisters, Eunice Kennedy Shriver, traveled the country visiting institutions for people with mental retardation. She was appalled by what she found. "Children and adults were housed in bleak, overcrowded wards of one hundred or more," she wrote, "living out their lives on a dead-end street, unloved, unwanted, some of them strapped in chairs like criminals. There was a complete lack of knowledge about their capacities. They were isolated because their parents were embarrassed and the public was prejudiced." Mrs. Shriver was determined to show the world that children and adults with mental retardation could lead active, rewarding lives.

During the 1960s Eunice Kennedy Shriver operated a summer camp for children with mental retardation at her home in Maryland. College students volunteered to teach swimming, gymnastics, basketball, and other sports. The campers made dramatic progress. Encouraged by this success, Shriver moved forward with her plans for a unique athletic competition for people with mental retardation.

In July 1968 one thousand athletes from twenty-six states and Canada gathered at Soldier Field in Chicago. Olympic medalist Rafer Johnson spoke at the Opening Ceremonies of the first International Special Olympics Summer Games. Today Special Olympics is a global organization that offers year-round training and competition for people with mental retardation. Every four years, the Special Olympics World Summer Games and World Winter Games are held. Summer

Eunice Kennedy Shriver helped open up the world of sports to many people with mental retardation.

events include swimming, bowling, roller-skating, horseback riding, and gymnastics. Among the winter events are downhill skiing, figure skating, speed skating, and floor hockey.

The winning Special Olympics athletes are awarded gold, silver, and bronze medals. But everyone who takes part in the games earns a ribbon. Special Olympics emphasizes participation more than competition. The oath, recited at every opening ceremony, embodies this spirit: "Let me win—but if I can't, let me be brave in the attempt."

A Special Olympics athlete receives her ribbon at an award ceremony.

Special Champions

In 1974 a young man named Curtis Leslie Thompson became a Special Olympics hero. He was battling cancer, and his doctors did not feel that he was strong enough to swim. Thompson was determined to compete. He carried away a silver medal and the admiration of thousands of spectators. Thompson died just five months later.

Like all athletes, Special Olympics athletes show fierce determination and dedication to their chosen sports. Some move beyond Special Olympics into more open competition. Jeffrey White entered his first Special Olympics swim meet when he was only eight years old. He continued to train as a swimmer and also earned a blue belt in karate. In addition, White is a gifted runner. In 1992 he ran in the Los Angeles **Marathon**, completing the 26.2-mile (42.2-kilometer) course in less than three hours. He finished as number 330 in a field of 20,000 participants.

Another outstanding Special Olympics athlete is Andy Leonard. Andy was born in Vietnam in 1969 during the Vietnam War. When he was three, he sustained a head injury

Breakfast of Champions

In the summer of 1999 Special Olympics athlete Nancy Filimonczuk was featured by the Kellogg's Cereal Company on its Wheaties box.

Andy Leonard was induced into the Special Olympics Pennsylvania Hall of Fame.

during a bombing attack on his village. At seven he came to the United States and was adopted by a family in Pennsylvania. His adoptive parents had faith in Andy's abilities, and enrolled him in a Special Olympics training program. Andy proved to have remarkable aptitude in **power lifting**, a sport that involves lifting a heavy weight. In the 1991 Special Olympics World Summer Games he placed first in the **bench-press** event. He was selected for the U.S. team in the regular Olympics in 1994. Leonard ranked second in the United States in his weight class.

Special Olympics gives its participants the chance to learn new skills, and to know the thrill of competition and achievement. As in any athletic endeavor, the rewards run far deeper. Paul Hoffman, a Special Olympics basketball medalist, explains, "Before I was really isolated and I really didn't have friends because no one wanted to be associated with a handicapped person. Then with Special Olympics I started feeling more confident about myself. . . . The most important message for people is that there's a place in this world for handicapped people outside Special Olympics. In the working world we can make a contribution." Hoffman went on to make his contribution as an equipment manager for a high school athletics program and as an inspirational public speaker.

Sam Komanici, a Special Olympics athlete from South Africa, summed it up in his address at the Opening Ceremonies for the 1999 Special Olympics World Summer Games: "The world may say I don't have a lot to give, but I have a gift to give you all here tonight. My gift is a gift of love. And I have another gift. It's the gift of friendship."

Special Olympics brings together athletes from all over the world.

Gunther Belitz demonstrates his athletic abilities in the high jump event.

Chapter Four

Going for the Gold

"Sport is a good way to communicate with other people and to get to know your body. Competitive sport is, to my mind, the challenge to move your body toward its limits. It can help you to accept a disability, to overcome prejudices toward disability, and to develop a self-confident identity."

—Gunther Belitz, German Paralympic medalist in track and field, 1992

Old Games, New Methods

Athletes with disabilities take part in every imaginable sport, from gymnastics

33

Ready! Set! Goal!

Rehabilitation specialists developed the game of goalball in West Germany after World War II as a sport for blinded veterans. Two teams, each with three players, defend goals at opposite ends of an indoor court. A bell inside the ball lets the players know where it is throughout the game. Since some blind people have partial vision, all of the players wear blindfolds to put everyone on an equal footing. Goalball is an exciting, fast-paced game that has become popular with blind athletes all over the world. "I like goalball's physical demands," says Jill Redfield, a member of the U.S. National Women's Goalball Team. "A player needs strength for throwing, agility for blocking, and plenty of **stamina**."

to basketball. In many cases, a disabled person can participate fully with nondisabled athletes, needing few, if any, special adaptations. For instance, when a blind wrestler meets a sighted opponent, his lack of vision is not a disadvantage. Because he and his opponent are in physical contact, the blind wrestler competes on an equal footing. He knows his opponent's exact position through the sense of touch.

In other instances, athletes with disabilities use special equipment and techniques. Blind bowlers use a portable metal railing. The bowler follows the railing with one hand to walk on a straight course as she prepares to roll the ball down the alley. A tiny battery-powered beeping device can be built into a standard baseball. In games of "beep baseball," blind players pitch, catch, and run the bases, always aware of the ball's location through its sound.

Amputees use special sporting prostheses. An athlete's prosthetic leg must be lightweight and extremely durable to withstand the stress of running. Sporting prostheses are made from **titanium**, a metal so strong it is used in airplane manufacture.

Athletes involved in wheelchair sports such as basketball and racing use specially designed sporting chairs. Sports chairs must be custom-built according to the owner's height and weight. In general the wheels are larger than those on a standard wheelchair, and the hand rims for turning the wheels are smaller. The seat is closer to the ground to cut wind resistance and increase speed.

Poised to Win

In order to move faster and make quick turns on the court, wheelchair basketball players often pump their upper bodies back and forth in rhythm with the turning wheels. Racers assume a position with high knees and flexed trunk. This posture lowers the athlete's center of gravity and increases speed.

Special wheelchairs have been designed to help athletes play sports.

When Diana Golden Brosnihan lost a leg to cancer at age twelve, she was afraid she would never be able to ski again. Then she discovered **slalom**, a form of skiing in which an athlete skis a zigzag course marked by a series of flags. For Brosnihan and other amputees slalom is a thrilling sport that presents unique challenges. One leg tires faster than two. Turns and bounces on the course cause added strain. One-legged slalom calls for heightened awareness and precision. "When I started people said, 'Isn't that wonderful! And so

Skiing presents some very exciting challenges for athletes with disabilities.

courageous!'" Brosnihan recalls. "But I didn't ski on one leg to be courageous. The commitment required to be an athlete is the same, whether all your body parts are working or not."

Among the Elite

The story appeared on the evening news in homes across the country—President Bill Clinton had gone jogging with a champion of the Boston Marathon. It was not unusual for the president to seek a photo opportunity with a celebrated athlete. But this time TV viewers were taken by surprise. Clinton's jogging companion was Jean Driscoll, one of the most outstanding wheelchair racers in the world.

Born with **spina bifida**, a condition that affects the spinal cord and nerves in the legs and pelvis, Jean Driscoll discovered wheelchair sports when she was sixteen. "I always thought wheelchair athletics would be second rate," she admitted years later. "You know—kind of soft and toned down. Then I watched my first wheelchair soccer game and I was hooked! People were zooming all over the field, tumbling out of chairs, climbing back in to keep playing. It was great! Nothing wimpy about it!" Driscoll won an athletic scholarship to the University of Illinois, where she trained as a racer. In 1990 she placed first in the women's wheelchair class at the Boston Marathon. She entered the Boston Marathon for the next six years and won every time. Driscoll became the first racer ever to win the Boston Marathon six years in a row.

Jean Driscoll crosses the finish line of the Boston Marathon. She won the women's wheelchair division race.

With her outstanding Boston Marathon performances, Jean Driscoll is regarded as an elite athlete. She is among the highly dedicated women and men who have won respect and recognition for disabled sports competition. The achievements of these athletes are admirable by any standards, regardless of disability.

Like Jean Driscoll, Chris Waddell has built his reputation in the arena of disabled sports. Paralyzed in a skiing accident when he was twenty, Waddell went on to win four silver and five gold medals as a skier in the Paralympic Winter Games. He skis slalom, using a low canvas wheelchair fastened to his ski. "It surprises people when I tell them that the quality of my life really hasn't diminished," Waddell declares. "I wasn't able to say I was the best at anything prior to my injury, and now I can, so in a sense it's a blessing."

Marla Runyan earned international acclaim in track-and-field events at the 1992 and 1996 Paralympics. She excelled at

the high jump and the 1500- and 5000-meter races. At the age of nine Runyan lost most of her vision due to an eye condition called **Stargardt's disease**. Though the runners around her are mostly a blur, she explains, "I can see the finish line. It's at the end of the straightaway." In 2000 Runyan became the first legally blind athlete to win a place on the U.S. Olympic team. She finished eighth in the women's 1500-meter dash.

Despite having lost most of her sight as a child, Marla Runyan became a member of the U.S. Olympic team.

Heights and Plunges

Like nondisabled members of the population, people with disabilities participate in an endless array of athletic activities. Not all disabled athletes are involved in formal competitions. Many are happy to compete against themselves, stretching their personal limits. Blind people, wheelchair users, and people with a range of other disabling conditions enjoy white-water rafting, horseback riding, hang gliding, skydiving, and similar challenges.

Testing the limits is a lifetime career for Olympian Kitty O'Neill, who is deaf. O'Neill is such an expert in diving, gymnastics, horseback riding, and other athletics that she built a career as a Hollywood stuntwoman. In scenes that require someone to leap from a building or tumble out of an airplane, O'Neill stands in for a film's less daring actress. She appeared in *Omen II*, *Airport*, and many other movies.

In May 2001, a teacher from Arizona set a unique world record. Erik Weihenmayer became the first blind climber to reach the summit of Mount Everest, the highest mountain on earth. Weihenmayer forms a mental map of the rock face above him by exploring with his hands and listening to descriptions given by his teammates. Before tackling Everest he had scaled several of the world's most formidable peaks, including Denali—also known as Mount McKinley—in Alaska, Mount Kilimanjaro in Tanzania, and Mount Aconcagua in Argentina.

Speed Record

In 1970 Kitty O'Neill broke the record for high-speed waterskiing, skimming over the water at a dizzying 104 miles per hour (167 kilometers per hour).

When he writes about climbing, Weihenmayer captures the excitement that fuels all athletes, whether or not they are challenged by disabilities. "A summit isn't just a place on a mountain," he explains. "A summit exists in our hearts and minds. It is a tiny scrap of a dream made real, indisputable proof that our lives have meaning. A summit is a symbol that with the force of our will and the power of our legs, our backs, and our two hands, we can transform our lives into whatever we choose them to be, whatever our hands are strong enough to create."

Erik Weihenmayer with his dog guide carries the torch for the 2002 Paralympics in Salt Lake City.

Jim Abbot played for several major league baseball teams, including the New York Yankees and the California Angels.

Chapter Five

A Level Playing Field

"When an obstacle of any kind pops up in your life, don't sit down and give up. You just have to keep on trying, and one day it will pay off. People who aren't afraid to meet a challenge are the real heroes in my book."

—Jim Abbott, former major league baseball player, born with one hand

The Meaning of Fairness

In the words of Casey Martin it sounds perfectly simple: "I always wanted to play professional golf and I thought I had the talent to do it, so I went ahead and did it." However, to officials at the Professional Golfers Association (PGA) there was nothing simple about Martin's situation. In fact, the case stirred so much controversy that it went all the way to the U.S. Supreme Court.

Casey Martin began to play golf when he was five, and over the years he became devoted to the game. Due to a rare disease called **Klippel-Trénaunay-Weber syndrome**, Martin has poor circulation in his right leg. The condition causes swelling and pain and makes it impossible for Martin to walk long distances. While he played golf at Stanford University, Martin was allowed to move around the course on an electric golf

Equal Access for All

The Americans with Disabilities Act (ADA) of 1990 was passed to ensure the civil rights of disabled people. The ADA states that reasonable accommodation shall be made wherever necessary to give disabled persons access to education, jobs, recreation, transportation, and public places. People with disabilities will not be denied access to any activity unless their participation fundamentally changes the nature of the activity in question.

cart. But the PGA required golfers to walk the course. When Martin asked to have the rule waived in his case, the PGA refused.

Martin sued the PGA under the Americans with Disabilities Act. In two lower courts he won his case. But the PGA appealed its case to the Supreme Court, the highest court in the nation.

Because of his illness, Casey Martin needs to use to a golf cart to play golf.

The PGA argued that if Martin used a cart while other golfers walked, he would have a competitive advantage. The PGA lawyers claimed that waiving the rule would fundamentally change the nature of the game. Martin's lawyers insisted that he was not asking to change the rules of the game. He was only asking to get to the game in order to play. "I really don't feel the cart gives me an unfair advantage," Martin told reporters. "If I had the chance to walk with a healthy leg or ride with a disability, it's not even close—I'd take the healthy leg every time."

In May 2001, the U.S. Supreme Court ruled in Casey Martin's favor. The PGA was forced to let him use a cart on professional golf tours. Some commentators were outraged. A sportswriter for *The Washington Post* demanded, "Where is it written that to play a sport at the most elite level is a constitutional right?" Yet many Americans applauded the court decision. They felt that Martin deserved the chance to play, to use his talents as fully as possible.

The concept of fairness lies at the heart of all competitive athletics. Sports organizations try to create "a level field" where the players can compete on an equal footing, but no two athletes are ever matched exactly. One athlete may have the advantage of greater agility while another may be able to make quicker decisions. Another competitor may have exceptional strength and endurance. Much of the suspense in sports comes from the complex interplay of these differing weaknesses and abilities. Which will win out—strength or speed?

The legal battle over Martin's use of a golf cart went all the way to the Supreme Court. The court decided in Martin's favor, and he was able to return to playing golf professionally.

Strategy or power? Perhaps there has never been a tr playing field, where all contestants are evenly matche

Where do accommodations for athletes with disal into this framework? When are special accommodat sonable, allowing the disabled athlete to compete fa the non-disabled? Can necessary accommodations tilt the playing field in the disabled athlete's favor? Are there situations when the participation of athletes with disabilities changes the very nature of the game? We are still seeking answers to these tangled questions. The Supreme Court ruled in favor of Casey Martin, but many more decisions remain to be made in the years ahead.

Where Do We Go from Here?

The 2008 Paralympic Games will be held in Bejing, China. Eight years in advance, Tommy Cornille and his parents began to prepare for this major event. With careful training, dedication, and a bit of luck, the Cornilles hope that Tommy will make the U.S. team.

Every four years the Paralympics attracts a wider audience. The games gather more and more corporate sponsors and secure increasing airtime on television. The general public is coming to realize that the Paralympics and other contests for

Making Marathon History

At the Boston Marathon, wheelchair racers are setting dramatic new records. In 1975 Bob Hall of the U.S. completed the course in 2 hours 58 minutes. In 2001 Ernst van Dyk of South Africa covered the distance in 1 hour 25 minutes, less than half Hall's time.

Thousands of people attended the closing ceremonies at the Paralympic Games in Sydney, Australia.

Athletes with disabilities continue to seek out new challenges and new opportunities to compete.

people with disabilities are a worthwhile spectacle, full of excitement and drama. Athletes with disabilities are constantly stretching the limits. They break old records and set new ones each year.

In addition, athletes with disabilities are finding ever greater acceptance in regular sporting events. Many disabled athletes move comfortably from specialized to regular sports, fully valuing both types of experience. Track-and-field star Marla Runyan has excelled in both arenas. "What Paralympians do is incredible," she states. "I don't want my message to be that every Paralympian can make it to the Olympic Games." She urges that all athletes be given opportunities to achieve at their peak and that their achievements be honored.

"Equality Through Sport" was the motto of the Silent Games for the Deaf in 1924. The concept still holds true as we move into the twenty-first century. Sporting events of every kind give athletes with disabilities the chance to excel. In a world where each individual is unique, these athletes draw upon their strengths and abilities to meet the challenges of competition.

Timeline

1889	William Hoy joins the Washington Nationals, becoming the first deaf player in major league baseball.
1924	The first International Silent Games for the Deaf are played in Paris.
1948	First Stoke-Mandeville Games for disabled veterans are held in Aylesbury, England.
1952	Lisel Hartel of Denmark is the first wheelchair user to compete in the Olympics.
1960	First Paralympics, limited to athletes with spinal-cord injuries, are held in Rome.
1968	First Special Olympics are held at Soldier Field in Chicago.
1976	U.S. Association of Blind Athletes (USABA) is founded.
1978	Cerebral Palsy International Sports and Recreation Association (CPISRA) is established.
1986	International Sports Federation for Persons with Mental Handicaps is chartered in The Netherlands.
1989	People of small stature found the Dwarf Athletic Association of the United States.
1990	President George Bush signs the Americans with Disabilities Act (ADA).
1994	Special Olympian Andy Leonard breaks world power-lifting record.
2000	Marla Runyan becomes the first legally blind athlete to earn a place on the U.S. Olympic team.
2001	U.S. Supreme Court rules that Professional Golfers' Association (PGA) must allow Casey Martin to use an electric cart on professional golf tours.

Glossary

amputation—absence or removal of a limb

bench press—a sport in which the athlete lifts a heavy weight while lying flat

cerebral palsy—a condition caused by damage to the brain, usually occurring at birth, which can affect speech and movement

congenital—present from birth

dressage—elaborate, formalized style of horseback riding

elite—of the highest class

epilepsy—a condition that can cause a range of symptoms, from momentary blackouts to convulsions

Klippel-Trénaunay-Weber syndrome—a rare disease that affects blood circulation, causing severe pain and swelling

marathon—a 26.2-mile (42.2-kilometer) race

mental retardation—impaired ability to learn or reason ranging from mild to profound

power lifting—a sport that involves lifting a heavy weight

priority—top concern

profoundly—at the greatest extreme

prosthesis—an artificial body part, such as a leg or hand

rehabilitation—training to help people with disabilities live independently and enter the job market

signing—to communicate by means of one of the many visual languages used by deaf people around the world

slalom–a type of skiing in which an athlete skis a zigzag course marked by a series of flags

spina bifida—congenital condition affecting the spinal cord and nerves of the lower body

stamina—endurance

Stargardt's disease—an eye condition that destroys central vision

titanium—a strong metal used in making sports prostheses

To Find Out More

Books

Caminski, Marty. *Fifteen Athletes Who Battled Back: Uncommon Champions*. Millbrook, CT: Boyds Mills, 2000.

Dinn, Sheila. *Hearts of Gold: A Celebration of Special Olympics and Its Heroes*. Woodbridge, CT: Blackbirch Press, 1996.

Runyan, Marla with Sally Jenkins and Maria Runyan. *No Finish Line: My Life as I See It*. New York: Putnam, 2001.

Savage, Jeff. *Top Ten Physically Challenged Athletes*. Springfield, NJ: Enslow, 2000.

Weihenmayer, Erik. *Touch the Top of the World: A Blind Man's Journey to Climb Farther than the Eye Can See*. New York: Dutton/Penguin, 2001.

Organizations and Online Sites

Disabled Sports USA (DSUSA), Far West Chapter
6060 Sunrise Vista Drive, #2540
Citrus Heights, CA 95610
http://www.dsusafw.org
This organization trains people with disabilities in a variety of sports, especially downhill skiing and waterskiing.

International Paralympic Committee
Adenauerallee 212-214
53113 Bonn
Germany
http://www.paralympic.org
Composed of 160 national committees and five disability-specific international sports federations, this organization runs the Paralympic Games.

National Disability Sports Alliance
5 West Independence Way
Kingston, RI 02881
http://www.ndsaonline.org
This national organization creates sporting events for people with cerebral palsy, traumatic brain injuries, and survivors of strokes.

Special Olympics
1325 G Street, NW, Suite 770
Washington, D.C. 20005
http://www.specialolympics.org
This organization provides sports opportunities and training through local organizations and sponsors international competition for people with mental retardation.

U.S. Association of Blind Athletes (USABA)
33 N. Institute Street
Colorado Springs, CO 80903
http://www.usaba.org
This organization sponsors local, state, and national competitions for blind athletes.

USA Deaf Sports Foundation
http://www.usadsf.org
This foundation develops sports activities for deaf athletes nationwide.

Wheelchair Sports USA
3595 E. Fountain Boulevard, Suite L-1
Colorado Springs, CO 80910
http://www.wsusa.org
This organization sponsors a variety of wheelchair sports at local, state, and national levels.

A Note on Sources

As I prepared to write this book, I turned to the extensive materials available from Special Olympics, Paralympics, USABA, CPISRA, and many other athletic organizations. Spokespersons from the local and national headquarters were eager to support this project and offered all the help they could. In addition, two full-length books proved extremely valuable. *Disability and Sport* by Karen P. DePauw and Susan J. Gavron provides a scholarly approach to the history and current structure of athletics for people with disabilities. *The First Twenty-five Years: Special Olympics* by Anna Bueno is a thoroughly researched and readable account of the development of this organization.

—*Deborah Kent*

Index

Numbers in *italics* indicate illustrations.

About the Author

Deborah Kent grew up in Little Falls, New Jersey, where she was the first totally blind student to attend the local public school. She earned a B.A. in English from Oberlin College and a master's degree from Smith College School for Social Work.

In 1975 Ms. Kent decided to pursue her lifelong dream of becoming a writer. She moved to San Miguel de Allende in Mexico. With the support of San Miguel's writing community she completed her first young-adult novel, *Belonging*, based on her experiences as the only blind student in a regular school. While living in San Miguel Ms. Kent helped to found the Centro de Crecimiento, the town's first school for children with disabilities.

Ms. Kent is the author of eighteen young-adult novels and more than fifty nonfiction titles. She lives in Chicago with her husband, children's author R. Conrad Stein, and their daughter Janna.